Simply Squares
by Sarah Wellfair

This is a technique I have been teaching for the last 6 years, It is quick, fun and very easy to do.

Simply squares does not rely on getting your points right or seams to match, stress free piecing.

They are all made from fat quarters as a starting point, three of the quilts have the same size finished squares, you could make two different ones and alternate them to make a bigger quilt.

They could also be made from scraps, have every square a different colour.

This works very well with plaids, checks and stripes, they always end up in the right position.

I would like to thank all the girls at the shop for helping and supporting me and at times listen to me moan a bit when things don't go well .

Thank you to Bryan Taphouse and Fabric Freedom for all the lovely fabrics in this book.

I hope you enjoy making these quilts as much as I enjoyed designing and making them.

Index

Simply Squares	Page 2
Simply Stained Glass	Page 4
Simply squares Double Trouble	Page 6
Sewing your blocks together quilt as you go	Page 8
Simply Squares Bag	Page 13
Simply Squares and Triangles	Page 16
Simply Squares Four patch	Page 18
Binding your quilt	Page 19
Spare Square Cushion	Page 20
Adding a Border	Page 21

Goose Chase Publishing
65 Great Norwood Street
Leckhampton
Cheltenham
Glos
GL50 2BQ
UK

Tel 01242 512639

ISBN 978-0-9555448-3-5

Printed By Frontier Print And Design
Tel 01242 573863

GW00497755

Simply Squares

Finished size approx without border 44 inches square.

Finished size with border approx 54 inches square.

Requirements.

Fabric 1   **1 fat quarter**
From this cut 9 pieces 3 1/2 inches square

Fabric 2   **1 Fat quarter**
From this cut 9 pieces 3 1/2 inches square

Fabric 3   **1 Fat quarter**
From this cut 9 pieces 4 1/4 inches square

Fabric 4   **1 Fat quarter**
From this cut 9 pieces 5 1/4 inches square

Fabric 5   **1 Fat quarter**
From this cut 9 pieces 6 1/2 inches square

Fabric 6   **1/2 metre**
From this cut 9 pieces 8 1/2 inches square.

Fabric 7 Framing   **3/4 metre**
Cut one pieces 11 1/4 inches by the width of your fabric (selvedge to selvedge)
Cut one piece 14 3/4 inches by the width of your fabric (selvedge to selvedge)

Border fabric   **1 1/2 metres**
This will do the front and the back of your borders

Backing fabric
2 1/2 metres or 9 fat quarters
From this cut 9 pieces 17 inches square.

Quilt as you go sashing and binding fabric
Quilt without a border   1 1/4 metres
Quilt with a border   1 1/2 metres

1 1/2 metres of warm and natural cotton wadding
From this cut 9 pieces 17 inches square and
4 pieces 5 inches by 56 inches for your borders

Thread to match for sewing and quilting

Rotary cutter mat and ruler

1. Take squares from fabric 2,3,4,5,6 and draw a line from corner to corner on the diagonal in both directions.
Using a rotary cutter make a small cut on the line in the centre of each square, between the marks.

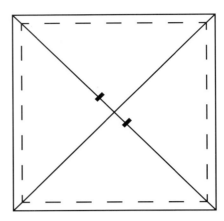

2. Place fabric 2 squares right sides together with fabric 1 squares and line up the edges.

Machine around the outside of the square with a 1/4 inch seam allowance.

Take sharp scissors and using the small cut you made earlier, cut the fabric 2 square on the lines out to the corners, be careful not to cut the other square.

3. Press the corner triangles away from the centre with the seam allowance towards the outer edge.

Be careful when pressing not to stretch the edges of the block.

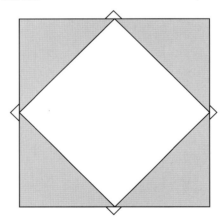

4. Take fabric 3 squares and place right sides together with the squares you have just made.

Stitch as before 1/4 inch seam around the outer edge.

Cut the top square as before on the drawn lines out to the corners and fold back the corners and press as before.

ur block should now look like this.

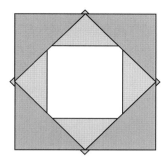

Place fabric 4 square on as before and stitch around em in the same way. Open and press.
rim blocks to 6 1/2 inches square at this point.

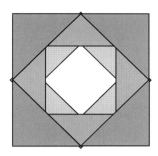

. Add fabric 5 squares stitch as before open and press.

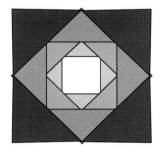

7. Add fabric 6 squares the same way.

8.All blocks are made in the same way.

9. They should now measure 11 1/4 inches square, you can trim them to size if needed.

Give them a good press being careful not to stretch the edges of your block as they are all on the bias

10. Take your contrast framing fabric strips and cut across them, cutting 18 pieces 2 1/4 inches by 11 1/4 inches and 18 pieces 2 1/4 inches by 14 3/4 inches.

11. Take the 11 1/4 inch strips and add on to the top and the bottom of each block with 1/4 inch seam allowance.

Press seam allowance toward the framing fabric.

12. Add the 2 1/4 inch by 14 3/4 inch framing strips to the other 2 sides and press the seam allowance towards the framing as before.

13.Blocks should now measure 14 3/4 inches square.
Layer blocks with wadding and backing squares and tack or spray baste in place for quilting.
14. Quilt as desired, I have quilted in the ditch around each square and lines in the framing 1/2 inch apart.
15. From Quilt as you go fabric cut down the length.
Cut 4 pieces 1 1/8 inches wide by the length for the front sashings.
Cut 4 pieces 2 inches wide by the length for the back sashings.
Follow instructions for quilt as you go.
If you are adding a border follow border instructions.

Bind quilt to finish

Simply Stained Glass
Finished Size approx 57 inches by 46 inches

Requirements
This Quilt is made up of 20 blocks 10 in one colour way and 10 in another.

Fabrics 1 and 2
Fat quarter of each   Centres of blocks
From each colour cut 10 pieces 3 ½ Inches square. 20 in total

Fabric 3 and 4
Fat quarter of each   Middle Triangles
From each colour cut 10 pieces 5 inches square. 20 in total

Fabric 5 and 6
½ Metre of each   Outer triangles
From each colour cut 10 pieces 7 7/8 inches square. 20 in total.

Fabric 7 Dark contrast framing
1 ½ Metres
From this cut the following pieces across the width of the fabric (selvedge to selvedge)
Cut one 3 ½ Inches by width
Cut one 5 Inches by width
Cut one 6 ¼ Inches by width
Cut one 7 7/8 Inches by width
Cut one 10 ¼ Inches by width
Cut one 11 ½ Inches by width

Fabric 8
Quilt as you go sashings and bindings
1 1/2 metre

Wadding   2 metres of warm and natural
Cut 20 pieces 13 Inches square

Backing   2 ½ Metres
Cut 20 pieces 13 Inches square

Thread to match for sewing and quilting
Sewing machine with ¼ Inch foot and walking foot

Cutting mat ruler and cutter

12 ½ Inch square

Sharp scissors

1. Take your 3 ½ Inch strip of dark contrasting fabric and cut across it into 35 pieces 1 ¼ Inches wide by ½ Inches. You will need 40 in total the rest can be cut later from the remaining fabric.

2. Do the same to the 5 inch strip of dark contrasting fabric.

Take your 3 ½ Inch squares and add one 3 ½ Inch strip to two opposite sides.

Press the seam allowance towards the dark contrast strip. Add the 5 inch strips to the other 2 sides and press in the same way.

4. Take the 5 inch squares and draw a line from corner to corner on the diagonal. Make a small cut with your cutter on the line in the centre between the marks.

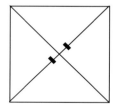 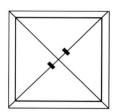

5. Place the square on top of your pieced square and line up the corners. Sew around the outside of the square with ¼ Inch seam allowance.

6. Using small sharp scissors cut on the lines out to the corners on the top square only. Open and press the triangles away from the centre square.

This square should now measure 6 ¼ Inches square. When pressing be careful not to stretch the outer edges as it is now on the bias.

7. Take your 6 ¼ Inch strip of dark contrast and your 7 7/8 inch strip and cut across it the same as before cutting 35 pieces from each.

Add the 6 ¼ Inch strips to 2 opposite sides as before and press towards the strip.

Add the 7 7/8 inch strips to the other 2 sides and press.

Take your 7 7/8 inch squares and mark from corner to corner as before and cut the centre as before.

). Place the square on top of the pieced square and sew ¼ Inch seam around the outside as before. Cut on the lines out to the corners open and press.

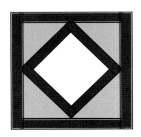

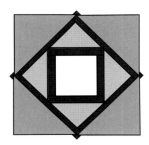

11. Take the last 2 dark contrast strips and cut into 35 pieces 1 ¼ Inches wide.

12. Add these strips as before. Press.

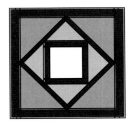

13. You should now have 17 blocks.

14. Cut the remaining dark contrast fabric into 1 ¼ Inch strips by the width of the fabric (Selvedge to selvedge) and cut from these.

5 pieces 3 ½ Inches
5 pieces 5 inches
5 pieces 6 ¼ Inches
5 pieces 7 7/8 inches
5 pieces 10 ¼ Inches
5 pieces 11 ½ Inches

These will complete the remaining squares.

15. Give all your blocks a final press, they should measure 11 1/2 inches square.

16. Layer with wadding and backing squares and pin, tack or spray baste in place.

17. Quilt as desired.
I have quilted mine in the dark contrast strips only.

18. Trim all wadding and backing from finished squares making sure they are all the same size. Mine were 11 1/4 inches after quilting and trimming.

From the quilt as you go sashing fabric

Cut 11 pieces 1 1/8 inches by the width of the fabric. (Selvedge to selvedge)
These are for the front quilt as you go sashings

Cut 11 pieces 2 inches by the width of the fabric (Selvedge to Selvedge)
These are for the back quilt as you go sashings.

Layout blocks in desired formation.

You should have 4 rows of 5 blocks.

Follow instructions for quilt as you go.

From remaining quilt as you go fabric cut 5 pieces 2 1/2 inches wide by the width of your fabric. Join them together end to end, fold these in half right sides out and press fold. These are to bind your quilt.

Bind quilt to finish.

Simply Squares Double Trouble
Finished size 43 inches square
53 inches square with a border
Requirements

Block 1
3 Fat quarters

Fat quarter 1
Cut 9 pieces 5 1/4 inches square
Fat quarter 2
Cut 9 pieces 5 1/4 inches square
Fat quarter 3
Cut 9 pieces 6 1/2 inches square

Block 2
3 Fat quarters

Fat quarter 1
Cut 9 pieces 5 1/4 inches square
Fat quarter 2
Cut 9 pieces 5 1/4 inches square
Fat quarter 3
Cut 9 pieces 6 1/2 inches square

Framing Fabric   3/4 metre
Cut one piece 11 1/4 inches by the width of your
fabric (selvedge to selvedge)
Cut one piece 14 3/4 inches by the width of your
fabric (selvedge to selvedge)

Border fabric   1 1/2 metres
This will do the front and the back of your borders

Backing fabric
2 1/2 metres or 9 fat quarters
From this cut 9 pieces 17 inches square.

Quilt as you go sashing and binding fabric
Quilt without a border   1 1/4 metres
Quilt with a border   1 1/2 metres

1 1/2 metres of warm and natural cotton wadding
From this cut 9 pieces 17 inches square and 4
pieces 45 inches by 56 inches for your borders
Thread to match for sewing and quilting

Rotary cutter mat and ruler

Working with block 1 fabrics.

1. Take the 5 1/4 inch squares of fabric 2 and the 6
1/2 inch squares of fabric 3 and draw a line from corner to corner on the diagonal in both directions.

Using a rotary cutter make a small cut on the line in
the centre of each square between the marks.

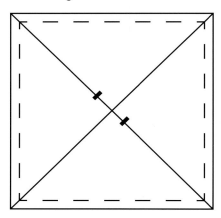

2. Place fabric 2 squares right sides together with
fabric 1 squares and line up the edges.

Machine around the outside of the square with a 1/4
inch seam allowance.

Take sharp scissors and using the small cut you made
earlier, cut the fabric 2 square on the lines out to the
corners, be careful not to cut the other square.

3. Press the corner triangles away from the centre
with the seam allowance towards the outer edge.

Be careful when pressing not to stretch the edges of
the block.

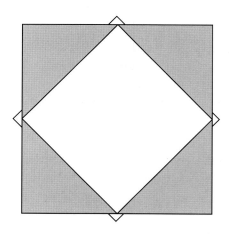

Take fabric 3 squares and place right sides together
with the squares you have just made.

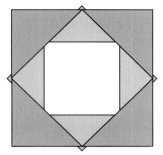

stitch as before 1/4 inch seam around the outer edge.

Cut the top square as before on the drawn lines out
to the corners and fold back the corners and press as
before.
This is block 1 finished.

5. Put these to one side and continue with block 2,
make them up in the same way.

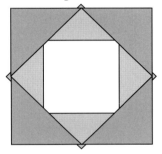 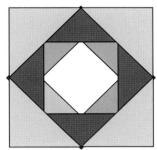

You should now have 18 blocks 9 in each colourway.

6. Take 5 of one colour and 4 of the other colour and
draw a line on the wrong side from corner to corner on
the diagonal in both directions.

7. Using your rotary cutter make a small cut on one of
the lines in the centre as you did before.

8. Take one of these blocks and place it right side together with one of the unmarked blocks of the opposite
colourway line up the corners and the centre of each
side and sew with quarter inch seam around the outer
edges as before.

9. Using sharp scissors cut on the lines out to corners
being careful not to cut the other block.

10. Open out the block and press seam allowance away
from the centre.

You should now have 9 blocks like this 5 with the
centres in one colour way and 4 centres in the opposite
colour way.

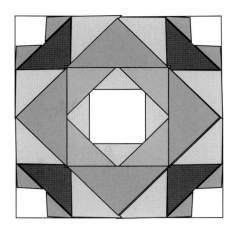

11. Take your contrast framing fabric strips and cut
across them, cutting 18 pieces 2 1/4 inches by 11
1/4 inches and 18 pieces 2 1/4 inches by 14 3/4
inches.

12. Take the 11 1/4 inch strips and add on to the
top and the bottom of each block with 1/4 inch
seam allowance.
Press seam allowance toward the framing fabric.

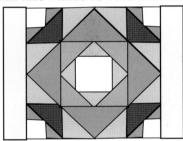

13. Add the 2 1/4 inch by 14 3/4 inch framing
strips to the other 2 sides and press the seam
allowance towards the framing as before.

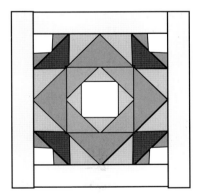

14. Quilt as desired. Trim back wadding and backing.
Cut 4 pieces 1 1/8 inches by width of fabric these
are your front quilt as you go sashings
Cut 4 Pieces 2 inches by width of fabric, these are
your back quilt as you go sashings.

Follow quilt as you go instructions.

Bind to finish.

Sewing your blocks together Quilt as you go

1. Trim all the quilted blocks to the same size.

2. Lat the blocks out in the desired formation. They will be joined in rows and then the rows joined together. The quilt as you go strips will be attached to the left hand side of the block. I always mark the side to be joined with a pin.

3. Take the 2 inch strips and fold them in half down the length.

4. take the first block and turn it over, wrong side up. Sew the folded 2 inch quilt as you go strip to the side with the pin in, raw edge to raw edge using 1/8th inch seam allowance.

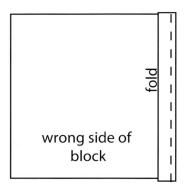

5. Turn the block over and place the 1 1/8th inch single strip right side down onto the front of your block on the same side as the double binding. Stitch the single strip with 1/4 inch seam allowance. Press isingle binding away from the block. You should now have both quilt as you go strips on the same edge back to back.

6. Place this block right side together with the one next to it and line up the single sashing with the right hand edge of your next block. Pin in place. I use plenty of pins for this to make sure it doesn't shift when sewing. Sew with 1/4 inch seam allowance. Join the rest of the blocks in the same way until they are all in rows.

7. Turn the row of blocks over and fold the back sahing over to cover the seam allowance and the previous stitch line, hand stitch in place.

8. leaving the top row of blocks, sew quilt as you go sashings to the top of row 2 the same as you have done for joining your blocks in rows. Press the front sashing away from the row of blocks.

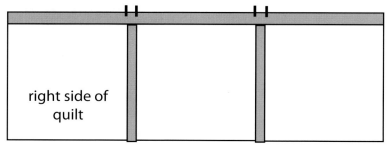

9. Using a ruler and pencil, mark in the seam allowance of the front sashing two marks for lining up the next row of blocks.

10 Pin the marks either side of the vertical sashing of the next row and then pin the blocks in between, this makes sure the sashings line up in both directions. Sew as before. Finish the back sashing as before.

11. If you are adding borders to your quilt follow instructions to make them up. Sew the quilt as you go sashings to the borders and then sew the borders to the quilt.

Simply Squares Bag
Made By Sarah Wellfair finished size approx 13 inches high 17 inches wide and
5 inches deep
This Bag is made with just 3 half metre pieces

Simply Squares and Triangles
Made by Sarah Wellfair Finished size 39 inches by 58 inches
Five fat quarters make these six blocks

Simply Squares Four Patch
Made By Sarah Wellfair finished size 44 inches square 54 with border
Simple squares and four patch units make up this block

Simply Squares
Made by Sarah Wellfair finished size 44 inches without border 54 inches with border

Simply Stained Glass
Made by Sarah Wellfair finished size 57 inches by 46 inches
Three Squares make up this simple block

Simply Stained Glass Reverse

Simply Squares Double Trouble

Made by Sarah Wellfair Finished Size 44 inches square approx. 54 inches with a border.
Blocks are made by sewing round only 6 squares ending with 25 pieces in each block.

Simply Squares Double Trouble Reverse

The back of this quilt was fat quarters of some of the fabrics used on the front.

...mply Squares Bag.

...alf metres of fabric.

...bric 1   Dark or Patterned
...ntres of squares
...t 3 strips 4 inches wide by width of fabric (Selvedge
...selvedge)
...om this cut
...t 24 pieces 4 inches square
...ter base of bag
...t 1 piece 18 inches by 6 inches
...ner base of bag
...t 1 piece 17 1/2 inches by 5 1/2 inches
...es to close bag
...t 1 piece 2 inches wide by width of fabric (Selvedge
...selvedge)

...abric 2   Medium patterned or plain
...ut 3 pieces 2 1/4 inches by width of fabric (Selvedge
... selvedge)

...ag lining
...ut 2 pieces 2 1/2 inches by 17 1/2 inches

...andles
...ut 2 pieces 22 inches by 5 1/2 inches
...hese can be longer or shorter if you want.

...inding for top of bag
...ut 2 pieces 2 1/2 inches by 17 1/2 inches

Fabric 3   Light patterned or plain
...ut 3 pieces 2 1/4 inches by width of fabric (Selvedge
...o selvedge)

Bag lining
...ut 2 pieces 11 1/2 inches by 17 1/2 inches.

Calico   1 metre
**1/2 metre of 90 inch wide warm and natural cotton
wadding**

Thread for sewing and quilting.

4 large wooden beads

Rotary cutter mat and ruler

---

1. Take your 2 1/4 inch strips of fabric 2 and 3 and sew them together right side together with a 1/4 inch seam allowance to make 3 pairs of strips. Press seam allowance towards the darker fabric.

2. It should now measure 4 inches wide.

3. From each of the units cut 8 pieces 4 inches square and one piece 8 inches by 4 inches.

4. Take your 4 inch pieced squares and draw a line on the diagonal from corner to corner on thr wrong side in both directions. Using your rotary cutter make a small cut on one of the lines in the centre of your block between marks.

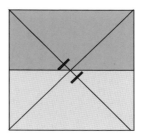

5. Place square right side together with dark 4 inch centre squares, carefully match up the corners and stitch around the outer edge with 1/4 inch seam allowance.

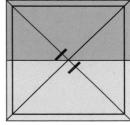

5. Using sharp scissors, insert them into the small cut you made earlier, cut the top block only out to the corners on the drawn line, be careful not to cut the other block.

6. Open and press triangles away from the centre careful not to stretch the edges as they are now on the bias.
Make all 24 blocks the same way

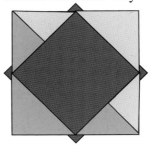

7. The bag has 12 blocks on both sides.

Layout blocks in desired pattern and sew together in 3 rows of 4 blocks.

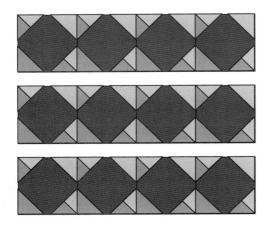

4. Press the seam allowance on row 1 and 3 in one direction and row 2 in the opposite direction.

5. Pin and sew the rows together carefully matching the seams.
Press the seams towards the top of the panel.
Make the other side of the bag the same way.

6. Take the outer base piece 18 inches by 6 inches and add to the bottom edge of both bag panels with 1/4 inch seam allowance.
Press seam allowance towards the base panel.

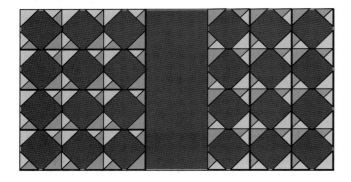

Cut a piece of wadding and calico approx 1 inch bigger than finished panel and sandwich together.

Pin, tack or spray baste in position and quilt.

Quilt in the ditch along the seams for the base, this will help when you make the bag up later.

I have quilted in straight lines on the base 1/4 inch apart and 1/4 inch in on all the dark centre squares.

Trim back wadding and calico to edges of bag.

7. Fold bag in half along the base and sew side sea with 1/4 Inch seam allowance matching up the squa at the sides.
Take one of the bottom corners of the bag and mat the side seam with centre base. Right side together This is the bottom corner section of bag

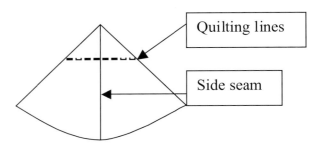

8. With the side seam on the top stitch across the quilting lines through the side and base to form the bottom of the bag. Do the same to the other corner. Corners can now be cut off leaving 1/4 Inch seam allowance.

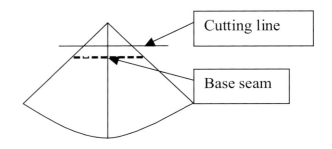

9. Turn the bag right side out.

10. **Making the handles**
Take your Handle strips and fold in half down the length right side out. Press fold.
Open out and fold raw edges into the centre fold you have just made. Press new folded edges.
Fold in half on original fold.

11. You should now have a strip a quarter the width of your original strip and with all raw edges hidden, open and place a 1 inch by 22 inch piece of wadding inside.
Stitch down the open edge first with 1/8 inch seam, then sew down the folded edge with 1/8 inch seam. Stitch down the middle with decorative stitching.
Fold the piece for the ties in the same way and stitch down both sides, cut it in half.

12. Pin the handles on the front of your bag 4 1/2 inches in from the side seams, with the handles facing down the bag, fold the tie in half and place the folded end in the middle of the bag panels and machine stitch in place.

r bag should now look like this.

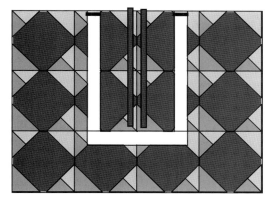

. Take the 3 peices 4 inches by 8 inches. Sew them
gether to make one panel with alternating fabrics.
is will be your pocket panel.

4. Cut a piece of wadding and calico the same size
 the pocket panel, lay the panel right side up on the
adding, now lay the calico on top of the panel stitch
cross the top edge and down the sides with 1/4 inch
eam allowance. Turn pocket right side out, roll the top
dge between your fingers until the seam is on the top,
ress and pin in place. Stitch 1/4 inch from this top
dge to hold in place.

5. Quilt pocket. I have quilted 1/4 inch either side of
ach seam.

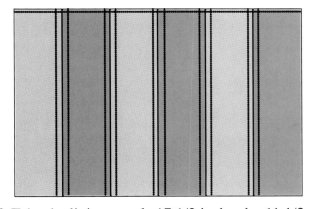

16. Take the lining panels 17 1/2 inches by 11 1/2
inches and find the centre of the long edge, I do this by
folding it in half, and pressing the fold.

Lay the pocket panel onto one of the lining panels
matching the centre seam of the pocket with the centre
of the lining on the bottom edge. Pin in place and stitch
down both sides of the pocket. I always reverse over
the top edge of the pockets for strength.

17. Add the 2 1/2 inch by 17 1/2 inch piece to the
bottom edges with 1/4 inch seam allowance.

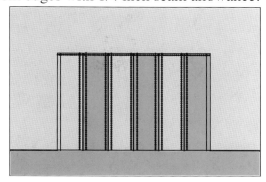

18. Add the 5 1/2 inch by 17 1/2 inch inner base
panel to the bottom edges of the bag panels.

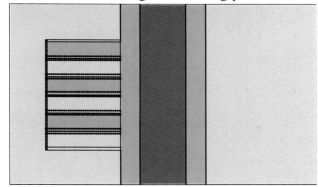

19. Place panel on wadding and calico and quilt.
Quilt in the ditch along the base panel.
20. Make up inner bag the same as for the outer
bag.
21. Place the lining inside the bag, carefully pin
around the top of the bag matching the side seams
first, use lots of pins.
Machine around the top with 1/4 inch seam.

22. Take your remaining 2 1/2 inches by 17 1/2
inches to bind the top of your bag.

Fold them in half down the length right sides out,
press the fold.

Unfold and place them right side together and stitch
across the short ends, refold. You should now have
a hoop of fabric.
Place the hoop of fabric on the top of the bag on the
outside with the raw edges together, line up and pin
the side seams first. Pin around the top of the bag
and make the binding hoop fit.
Stitch in place by machine with a generous 1/4 inch
seam.
Fold binding hoop over the top and slip stitch
the folded edge down to the lining covering any
previous stitching.
Thread Beads onto ties and make a knot in the
ends.

Simply Squares and Triangles
Finished Size approx 39 inches by 58 inches.
Requirements

Fabric 1   1 Fat Quarter
Centre of your blocks
Cut 6 pieces 4 1/2 inches square
Fabric 2   1 Fat Quarter
First triangles
Cut 2 pieces 3 1/2 inches by 21 inches
Fabric 3   1 Fat Quarter
First triangles
Cut 2 pieces 3 1/2 inches by 21 inches
Fabric 4   1 Fat Quarter
Second triangles
Cut 3 pieces 5 1/2 inches by 21 inches
Fabric 5   1 Fat Quarter
Second triangles
Cut 3 pieces 5 1/2 inches by 21 inches
Fabric 6   1 metre
Framing fabric
From this cut 22 pieces 1 1/2 inches wide by the
width of the fabric (selvedge to selvedge)
From these cut the following
Cut 12 pieces 4 1/2 inches by 1 1/2 inches
Cut 12 pieces 6 1/2 inches by 1 1/2 inches
Cut 12 pieces 8 1/2 inches by 1 1/2 inches
Cut 12 pieces 10 1/2 inches by 1 1/2 inches
Cut 12 pieces 14 inches by 1 1/2 inches
Cut 12 pieces 16 inches by 1 1/2 inches
Fabric 7   1 metre
Second Framing
From this cut 12 pieces 2 1/2 inches by the width of
your fabric (selvedge to selvedge)
From these cut the following.
Cut 12 pieces 16 inches by 2 1/2 inches
Cut 12 pieces 20 inches by 2 1/2 inches
Fabric 8   3/4 metre
Quilt as you go and binding fabric
Cut 4 pieces 1 1/8 inches by width of fabric.
Cut 4 pieces 2 inches by width of fabric.
Binding.
Cut 5 pieces 2 1/2 inches by width of fabric
Wadding   1 1/4 metre of 90 inch wide
warm and natural cotton wadding
Cut 6 pieces 22 inch square.
Backing   1 3/4 metres
Cut 6 pieces 22 inches square.
Thread for sewing and quilting
Rotary cutting mat ruler and cutter.

1. Take your 4 1/2 inch squares and add a 1 1/2 inch
by 4 1/2 inch framing to the top and bottom of your
square. Press seam allowance towards the framing

2. Add the 6 1/2 inch by 1 1/2 inch framing to the
other 2 sides and press as before.

3.Take your 3 1/2 inch strips of fabric 2 and 3 and
sew them together right side together with a 1/4 inch
seam allowance to make 2 pairs of strips. Press seam
allowance towards the darker fabric.

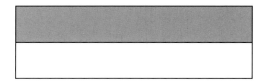

It should now measure 6 1/2 inches wide.

From each of the units cut 3 pieces 6 1/2 inches
square.

4. Take your 6 1/2 inch pieced squares and draw a
line on the diagonal from corner to corner in both
directions. Using your rotary cutter make a small cut
on one of the line in the centre of your block between
the marks.

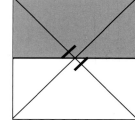

5. Place square right side together with centre
squares, carefully match up the corners and stitch
around the outer edge with 1/4 inch seam allowance.

Using sharp scissors, insert them into the small cut made earlier, cut the top block only out to the corners on the drawn line, be careful not to cut the other block.

Open and press triangles away from the centre careful not to stretch the edges as they are now on the bias. Make all 6 blocks the same way. Square block to 8 1/2 inches.

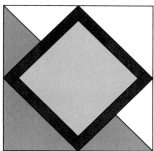

Take your 8 1/2 inch framing fabrics and add to the top and the bottom of your blocks. Press as before and add the 10 1/2 inch framings to the other 2 sides.

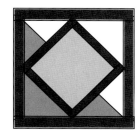

. Take your 5 1/2 inch strips of fabric 4 and 5 and sew them together right side together with a 1/4 inch seam allowance to make 3 pairs of strips. Press seam allowance towards the darker fabric.
From these cut 6 pieces 10 1/2 inch square.
Draw a line on the diagonal from corner to corner in both directions. Using your rotary cutter make a small cut on one of the lines in the centre of your block between the marks.

10. Place square right side together with centre squares, carefully match up the corners and stitch around the outer edge with 1/4 inch seam allowance. Cut open on the lines as before and press away from the centre.

Measure your blocks they should measure 16 inches. Trim to size if necessary

11. Add the remaining framings in the same way. Press seam allowance towards the framing.

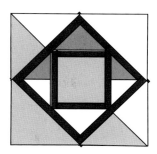

12. Take the 2nd framing fabrics and add the 2 1/2 inch by 16 inches to the top and bottom of your block. Press seam allowance towards the framing.

13. Add the remaining framing strips to the other 2 sides and press as before.

14. Sandwich squares with wadding and backing and pin, tack or spray baste in place.

15. Quilt squares as desired.
I have quilted in the inner framings and 1/2 inch inside the triangles.
The outer framings I have quilted around the framing 2 lines 1/2 inch apart.
16 Trim wadding and backing away and trim all blocks to the same size, mine were 19 1/2 inches square.

Follow instructions for quilt as you go.

Bind to finish

Simply Squares four Patch
Finished size approx without border 44 inches square.
Finished size with border approx 54 inches square.

Fabric 1	**1 Fat Quarter**

Centre Square
Cut 9 pieces 5 1/4 inches square

Fabric 2	**1 fat quarter**

First 4 patch
Cut 3 pieces 2 7/8 inches by the 22 inches

Fabric 3	**1 Fat quarter**

First 4 patch
Cut 3 pieces 2 7/8 inches by the 22 inches

Fabric 4	**1 Fat Quarter**

Second 4 patch
Cut 3 pieces 3 1/2 inches by 22 inches

Fabric 5	**1 Fat Quarter**

Second 4 patch
Cut 3 pieces 3 1/2 inches by 22 inches

Fabric 6	**1/2 metre**

Outer Triangles
Cut 9 pieces 8 1/2 inches square

Fabric 7	**3/4 metre**

Framing
Cut one piece 11 1/4 inches by the width of your fabric (selvedge to selvedge)
Cut one piece 14 3/4 inches by the width of your fabric (selvedge to selvedge)

Fabric 8
Quilt as you go sashings and bindings
Quilt without a border	1 1/4 metres
Quilt with a border	1 1/2 metres

Wadding
1 1/2 metres of warm and natural cotton wadding
From this cut 9 pieces 17 inches square and
4 pieces 45 inches by 56 inches for your borders
Thread to match for sewing and quilting

Border fabric	**1 1/2 metres**

This will do the front and the back of your borders

Backing fabric
2 1/2 metres or 9 fat quarters
From this cut 9 pieces 17 inches square.

1. Take your 2 7/8 inch strips of fabric 2 and 3 and join them in pairs down the length with a 1/4 inch seam allowance. Press seam towards the darker fabric . Make 3, from these cut 18 pieces 2 7/8 inch by 5 1/4.

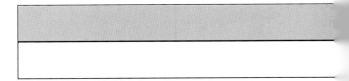

2. Take 2 of these units and place them right sides together alternating the colours. Carefully match the centre seam. Sew with 1/4 inch seam. Make 9 of this unit. They should now measure 5 1/4 inches square.

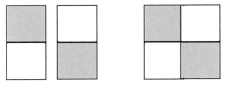

3. Take the 3 1/2 inch strips of fabric 4 and 5 and do the same again and make 9 four patch units 6 1/2 inches square.

4. Take all the four patch units and draw a lines on the diagonal on the wrong side, in both directions. Make a small cut in the middle on one of the lines with your rotary cutter between the marks.

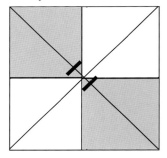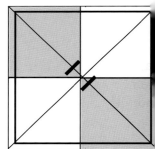

5. Place pieced Square onto centre square right sides together. Sew 1/4 inch seam allowance around the outside edge. Using sharp scissors cut on the lines out to the corners being careful not to cut the middle square.
Open out and press seams away from the centre.

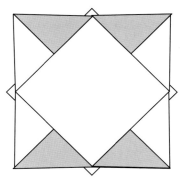

our blocks should now measure 6 1/2 inches if
are a little bigger trim to size.

the 6 1/2 inch four patch unit in the same way.

n and press as before. It should measure 8 1/2
hes trim to size if necessary.

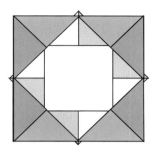

Take the 8 1/2 inch squares and draw the diagonal
es on the wrong side and make a small cut in the
ntre on the line as before. Place the square right
les together with the pieced blocks and stitch 1/4
ch seam around the outer edge.

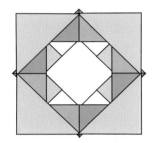

ake you contrast framing fabric strips and cut across
em, cutting 18 pieces 2 1/4 inches by 11 1/4 inches
nd 18 pieces 2 1/4 inches by 14 3/4 inches.

2. Take the 11 1/4 inch strips and add on to the top
nd the bottom of each block with 1/4 inch seam al-
owance.
Press seam allowance toward the framing fabric.

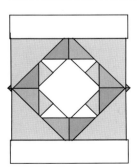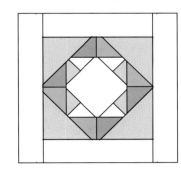

13. Add the 2 1/4 inch by 14 3/4 inch framing strips to
the other 2 sides and press the seam allowance towards the framing as before.

14. Quilt as desired. Trim back wadding and backing.
Cut 4 pieces 1 1/8 inches by the length of fabric
these are your front quilt as you go sashings
Cut 4 Pieces 2 inches by the length of fabric, these
are your back quilt as you go sashings.

If you are adding a border you will need 8 of each
size.

Cut 4 pieces 2 1/2 inches for binding your quilt.

Follow quilt as you go instructions.

Bind to finish.

Binding your quilts.

There are many ways to bind your quilt, all of them are
good, I usually do a square end binding as I find I can
get my quilt flatter this way.

You may need to join strips to get them long enough.

Fold your binding strips in half right side out down the
length. Press fold.

Measure the quilt through the middle from side to side
and cut 2 bindings to this size. Pin one binding raw edge
to raw edge on the top edge of the front of your quilt and
stitch in place with 1/4 inch seam allowance. Repeat for
the bottom edge.

Turn each binding over to the back of your quilt and slip
stitch in place by hand covering the stitch line.

Measure the quilt through the middle top to bottom and
add 1 1/2 inches to this measurement, cut the other 2
binding strips to this size. Pin one to each side of the
front of your quilt leaving 3/4 inch overlap top and bottom, sew as before.

Fold the short overlap to the back of your quilt on each
end. Fold binding to the back of your quilt and slip stitch
as before. Repeat for the other side.

Your quilt is now ready to be signed and dated.

Spare Square Cushion

When you have finished your quilt you very often have fabric left over, why not make another spare block and make it into a cushion.

Any Size you like.

Take any size block, trim it square if necessary. Decide what finished size you want your cushion to be. Take the measurement of your block minus the seam allowance away from this. 14 1/2 inch block is 14 inches without seam allowance

Finished size required	18 inches
Block size	14 inches
	------------
	4 inches

Divide this by 2 and add 1/4 for seam allowance, this is the width of your border.

The length for the first 2 are the same as your block size. 14 1/2 inches by 2 1/4 inches add these to the top and bottom of your block.

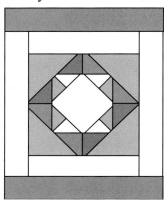

Measure through the middle and cut the other 2 border strips to this length. 18 inches by 2 1/4 inches.

Add these to the other 2 sides.

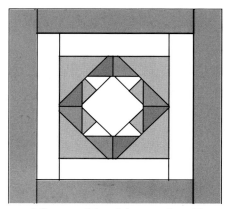

Place on wadding and backing and quilt.

Trim back wadding and backing to edges of panel.

Back of Cushion

Zips are by far the best way to finish your cushions Buy a zip that is 2 inches bigger than your cushion, doing this you don't need to sew around the zipper head.

It is easier to put the zipper 3 inches down from one edge of the cushion than it is to put it in the seam.

Take the size of the cushion panel and take 3 inches from this measurement.

Panel Size	18 inches	by	18 inches
			-3 inches
			------------
	18 inches	by	15 inches
Add seam allowance			1 1/2 inches

Cut size	**18 inches by**		**16 1/2 inches**
Other piece will be	18 inches by		3 inches
Add seam allowance			1 1/2 inches

Cut size	**18 inches by**		**4 1/2 inches**

Take the 18 inch by 16 1/2 inch back panel and fold in 1/2 inch down one of the long sides and press fold stitch with 1/4 inch seam. Do the same to the long side of the other backing pieces. These are you zipper edges.

On the same 2 edges fold over 1 inch and press again

Take your zipper and the larger back panel and pin the folded edge right side up as close to the Zipper teeth as you can get, starting 2 inches in from the zipper head. Leaving the zipper closed and using your zipper foot stitch as close to the folded edge as you can get.

Now take the other piece and place the folded edge over the zipper teeth covering the first row of stitching and pin in place. Using you zipper foot stitch down this side as close as you can get to the zipper.

Move the zipper head to the centre. Close the open end and stitch across to close.

Lay backing panel right side down and place the cushion panel on top right sides up.